Committee of the banks of the cities of New York

The silver question

Memorial to Congress, January, 1878

Committee of the banks of the cities of New York

The silver question
Memorial to Congress, January, 1878

ISBN/EAN: 9783337233761

Printed in Europe, USA, Canada, Australia, Japan

Cover: Foto ©Suzi / pixelio.de

More available books at **www.hansebooks.com**

XX.

DUTY OF THE GOVERNMENT.

It is the duty of the Government to provide a satisfactory currency. In order that it may be satisfactory, it must first work equal justice to all interests; next, it must be safe; and lastly, it must be convenient. No currency can be good that does not combine these qualities. The equal combined use of both precious metals will distribute impartial justice to the producers and owners of both; the supply of both metals will double the basis of redemption, and thus enhance safety; the two metals will make up for each others deficiencies, and thus promote convenience. The advocate of gold and the advocate of silver should not, either of them, ask for too much; let them be just to each other, and both may safely abide the results. When cometallism shall have prevailed for a time, these powerful contestants may find that, even from a selfish point of view, their interests can best be promoted by mutual concession. All minor considerations should give way to the great interests of the people; for thus only can private as well as public welfare be best conserved.

Pittsburgh, Penna., November, 1885.

ECONOMIC MONOGRAPHS. *No. II*

THE

SILVER QUESTION

THE DOLLAR OF THE FATHERS

VERSUS

THE DOLLAR OF THE SONS

BY

DAVID A. WELLS

NEW YORK

G. P PUTNAM'S SONS

182 FIFTH AVENUE

1878

Works on Political Economy.

THE WEALTH OF NATIONS. An enquiry into the Nature and Causes of. By ADAM SMITH. 12mo, cloth extra, 792 pages . $2 00

A perennial work, and the only book in history to which has been accorded the honor of a Centenary Celebration.

ESSAYS ON POLITICAL ECONOMY. By FREDERICK BASTIAT, with Introduction and Notes by DAVID A. WELLS. 12mo, cloth $1 25

" The laws of an abstruse science have never been made more clear, or expressed more forcibly."—*Cincinnati Commercial.*

THE SOPHISMS OF PROTECTION. By FREDERICK BASTIAT, with Introduction by HORACE WHITE. 12mo, cloth extra, 400 pages $1 00

"Contains the most telling statements of the leading principles of Free-Trade ever published."—*N. Y. Nation.*

WHAT IS FREE-TRADE? An Adaptation for American Readers of Bastiat's " Sophism of Protection." By EMILE WALTER, a Worker. 12mo, cloth 75

" Unsurpassed in the happiness of its illustrations."—*N. Y. Nation.*

SOCIAL ECONOMY. By Prof. J. E. THOROLD ROGERS. Revised and edited for American readers. 12mo, cloth . . . 75

"Gives in the compass of 150 pages. concise, yet comprehensive answers to the most important questions in social economy * * * cannot be too highly recommended for the use of teachers, students, and the general public."—*American Athenæum.*

PROTECTION AND FREE-TRADE. A series of essays. By ISAAC BUTTS. 12mo, cloth extra $1 25

" A clear and effective presentation of the case."—*N. Y. Evening Post.*

AN ALPHABET IN FINANCE. A simple statement of permanent principles, and their application to questions of the day. By GRAHAM MCADAM. With Introduction by R. R. BOWKER. 12mo, cloth, $1 25

" A timely volume whose directness and raciness can but be of service."—*New Englander*
" A model of clear-thinking and happy expression."—*Portland Press.*

SUMNER (Prof. W. G., of Yale College) **Lectures on the History of Protection in the United States.** Octavo, cloth extra 75

" There is nothing in the literature of free-trade more forcible and effective than this little book."—*N. Y. Post.*
" The book is especially timely, because it furnishes an adequate application of the principles of economic science to the conditions existing in this country."—*Buffalo Courier.*

WELLS (DAVID A.) **How shall the Nation Regain Prosperity?** A Discussion of the elements and amount of our National Wealth, and the causes and remedies for the present industrial, commercial, and financial depression. 8vo, cloth. (In preparation).

STURTEVANT (Prof. J. M.) **Economics, or the Science of Wealth.** A TREATISE ON POLITICAL ECONOMY, for the use of High Schools and Colleges, and for the general reader. Octavo, cloth.

(In Press.)

THE
SILVER QUESTION

THE DOLLAR OF THE FATHERS

VERSUS

THE DOLLAR OF THE SONS

ALSO

AN EXTRACT FROM AN ARTICLE IN THE NORTH AMERICAN
REVIEW, NOVEMBER, 1877,
ON THE UNCONSTITUTIONALITY OF THE REPEAL OF THE
OBLIGATIONS OF THE RESUMPTION ACT

BY

DAVID A. WELLS

NEW YORK
G. P. PUTNAM'S SONS
182 FIFTH AVENUE
1877

THE substance of this inquiry appeared originally in the columns of the Cincinnati *Commercial,* July 2d, 1877, in the form of a letter addressed to the editor, Murat Halstead, Esq. A continued demand for it in a more permanent and readable shape, and the continued interest on the part of the public in Europe as well as the United States, on the question of the future use of silver as a material for coinage, have induced its present republication, with such additions and amendments as a further and larger consideration and examination of the subject have suggested.

THE AUTHOR.

NORWICH, CONN., December, 1877.

THE SILVER QUESTION.

WHAT KIND OF CURRENCY OUR COUNTRY NEEDS.

SHALL WE LOOK FORWARD OR BACKWARD?

WHY THE CHINESE DO NOT COIN THE PRECIOUS METALS.

IN China the Government long ago ceased to coin the precious metals or regulate " the value thereof." Gold in China is not money. Silver is money; but neither are coined. Both are merchandise, and pass by weight and fineness. But although the Chinese Government has abandoned the coinage and regulation of the value of the precious metals, it has not absolutely and entirely abandoned all coinage.

It provides one coin, and one only, for the use of

its people, namely, an ugly, coarse and comparatively heavy disk, composed mainly of iron, with a little copper; cast, and not stamped, and bearing some rude characters, letters or signs upon its surfaces. This coin, which is known among foreigners by the name of *cash*, has a value of about one mill, American money, and is made with a hole in the center for convenience of stringing in tens and its decimal multiples. It occasionally drifts into the regions of Western civilization, and doubtless often suggests the inquiry, "How can any people use a coin so heavy and of such trifling value to any advantage in making their exchanges?" The answer is a very simple one. The wages of manual labor in China do not in general exceed 15 or 20 cents per day (our money); and these wages serve for the support and tolerable comfort of the great mass of the people, because, in part by reason of the great stability of values, but mainly because of the fact that labor itself is the real standard of value, to which the prices of all the products of labor adjust themselves; so that in China, upon apparently small wages, a man may live as well as in other countries upon nominally larger wages. But whatever may be the wages of a day in any country, they must be capable of division into many parts, in order to be exchanged for the many necessities of an individual or a family. In most countries this division is effected by the use of coined (metallic) money. But with wages at 20 cents per day, the use of coined gold would obviously be impracticable. The equivalent of a day's labor in gold would be too small to be handled conveniently; the equivalent of an hour's labor in gold would be no bigger than a pin's head. And in a smaller degree would be also the inconvenience of using coined silver for effecting the division of wages ruling at the rate of 15 to 20 cents per day. A quarter day's wages would be represented by a silver coin not so large as our 5-cent piece; and an hour's wages, which in turn might buy a pound of rice, and perchance a chopstick to eat it with, by a piece of silver no larger in circumference than the flat surface of a small split pea. Therefore the Chinese intelligently discard the use of coined gold and silver, and in their place have substituted the bulky and cheap, but at the same time admirable, because well adapted and useful *cash*, which sustains the same relations to their low nominal wages and prices that gold and silver coin sustains to the nominally high wages and prices of other countries; 200 pieces of *cash* dividing a day's wages of 20 cents into 200 equal parts for convenience in exchange for commodities and for the payment of taxes, estimated by a correspondingly low standard. Now all this comprises a lesson of experience, which those interested in the question to what extent can or shall silver be made the circulating medium, and an instrumentality of exchange in the United States, may do well to consider.

8 THE SILVER QUESTION.

1792 AND 1877.

Eighty-five years ago (when the dollar of the fathers was first established) the average price of the ordinary labor of adult males was not in excess of 40 and 45 cents per day. [The pay of soldiers in the army was $4 per month, and one ration per day of the value of 12 cents. The military storekeeper at Springfield, Mass., received $40 per month; artificers and armorers at posts on the frontier, $5 per month; United States District Judges, $1,000 per annum; messengers in the Government offices, $150 per annum.] The prices of all commodities, conforming then as now to the prices of labor, were also correspondingly small, while cash transactions were exceedingly limited. The fathers, moreover, were a stay-at-home people, and made but few journeys, or journeys of any considerable distance. Under such circumstances, the gravity of silver was a matter of very little consequence, and a bulky, cumbersome coinage (the dollar of the fathers) was not then an inconvenient instrumentality for making exchanges, and for the same reason that the heavy cheap Chinese *cash* is not an inconvenient instrumentality for making the present retail Chinese exchanges.

The present condition of affairs, comparing 1877 with 1790, or with even 1840, a period of fifty years later, is, however, entirely different. The prices of labor and of its products have greatly advanced. [The pay of soldiers in the army is $13 per month, and one ration. The military storekeeper at Springfield, Mass., receives $200 per month ; armorers, from $1.75 to $3.50 per day; United States District Judges, $4,000 per annum ; messengers in Government offices, $750 to $1,000 per annum.] Now everybody travels. Comparatively, and probably absolutely, more people go every year from the Atlantic to the Pacific, and *vice versa*, than fifty years ago went from State to State. Negroes now travel in the Southern country ten times as much probably as did all the people in that section before the Revolution. Now cash transactions are numerous and often very extensive. Everybody carries more or less money in his pocket and it is far from unusual for individuals to carry habitually as much as $100 on their persons. No one would think of starting upon any considerable journey with any less sum of money at his immediate command. Under such circumstances the weight or " tonnage" of silver becomes an element the importance of which has thus far been overlooked in considering the extent to which this metal can in future be used as currency.

THE WEIGHT OF SILVER.

Eighteen dollars and fourteen cents, represented by the present subsidiary silver coinage of the United States, weigh a pound ; one hundred dollars weigh five and a half pounds, and for every thousand dollars that a man is paid in silver, a wheelbarrow would become necessary if he proposed to remove it. The wheelbarrow, in fact, will become the essential, and possibly the fashionable, portemonnaie for all who propose to engage in any considerable moneyed transactions, if the dollar of the fathers is to be made by law the principal circulating medium. If a business was extensive, and it became desirable to pay at once $300,000 (in the dollar of the fathers), then the wheelbarrow would have to be discarded, and the railroad car called into requisition.* And if silver is to be made the basis of banking, it is well to consider that there is not probably a bank vault in the country that can hold and sustain a single million of coined silver weighing more than twenty-five tons. If silver is to become our practical single standard, a new style of bank architecture must be adopted.

---

* The following table, prepared for the writer by Mr. E. B. Elliott, of the United States Treasury Department, represents the weights in pounds avoirdupois of various sums of United States silver coinage :

Number of dollars.	Weight in pounds avoirdupois.
100	5.51
1,000	55.12
10,000	551.16
30,000	1,653.47
50,000	2,755.78
100,000	5,511.55
300,000	16,534.66

RELATION OF NATURAL LAWS AND NATIONAL NECES-
SITIES TO THE SILVER PROBLEM.

While silver, therefore, is not an inconvenient coin in
countries of low prices and limited internal exchanges,
and however it may once have favorably answered to
conditions in the United States, our present condition
of affairs—our high nominal wages and prices, and the
necessity that exists for the carrying of comparatively
large sums of money upon the person—would obviously
seem to preclude the possibility of its use for the bulk
of even the retail business of the country. And if by
law silver should now be made the exclusive standard
for money values in the United States, no law could en-
force its use for general circulation. Substitutes of paper
money would be resorted to and speedily replace it.

Again, if it is proposed to do business with all the
world on terms of equality—and the great trouble with
us as a nation to-day is, that by reason of various circumstances we are not so able, and, therefore, cannot
dispose of the excess of our commodities—we must
make use of those instrumentalities of trade of every kind
(ships, engines, railways, and more especially the money)
which the commercial world has adopted. Now the
money of the commercial world, of all international
trade, is mainly gold ; and the United States has little
commerce with any country which uses a silver standard. To some this may appear as a matter of very

little importance ; but this opinion will not long be en-
tertained if it is remembered that so sharp is the competition of various countries for trade, and so complete-
ly have the barriers of space and time been broken
down by the steamship, the railroad, and the telegraph,
that the question as to who shall take the lead in sup-
plying the world with certain great commodities is
going to turn in the future, not on cents, but on frac-
tions of cents, per yard, pound, or bushel; and that the
opportunity for employment and for the earning of a
comfortable livelihood may be denied to thousands by
the apparently trifling fluctuations in the purchasing
power or the inconvenience of the money which the
country may use in making its exchanges.

And if the American laborer—if the masses of our
people, now distressed, now seeking employment, and
painfully realizing that in the midst of abundance we
cannot market our abundance, and because we cannot market it production stops and poverty increases—
could also realize how much of all this trouble is con-
nected with the attempt to make the United States
adopt and use forms of money, or media of exchange,
which our own experience and the experience of other
nations teaches we should not use, the advocacy of
anything but most stable, non-fluctuating, and commer-
cially valuable currency would be anything but popular.

As a condition of national defense, furthermore—to
enable the nation to carry on a future war, foreign or

domestic, offensive or defensive—a full supply of the most valuable coin that is purchasable and salable without discount in other countries (and so available for settling international balances) is more necessary than a full supply of arms, ships, or forts. And the safest depositories of such coin are not the vaults of banks or of the Federal Treasury, but the pockets of the people ; and the conveniences of the people would prompt them to employ more coin, and so keep up a greater supply of the essential munition of war, if gold was the standard, than if the standard was exclusively a commodity so cumbersome as silver.

But the remonetization of silver, or the proposed resstoration of the "dollar of the fathers," if silver continues depreciated, would be equivalent to abolishing the use of coin to any large extent as a circulating medium ; or, in other words, natural laws have ordained that the use of silver, in any highly prosperous commercial community, shall be limited to its use as a subsidiary token coinage ; while sound policy and the dictates of national interest require that it shall not be made legal tender except as a token currency for small amounts.

REMONETIZATION OF SILVER A QUESTION OF NATIONAL CONVENIENCE.

Remonetization of silver is, therefore, a question of convenience, of tonnage, of gravity, and cost of trans-

portation. The kind of coin a country should have
and use must depend upon the value of its transactions,
the prices of its labor, and the rapidity and magnitude
of its exchanges. Iron was not ill adapted to Sparta
as a metal for coinage. It would not, however, suit
Chicago ; and everybody in Chicago and elsewhere who
will take the trouble to understand why it would not
suit, will at the same time see that it is not the dollar of
the Spartan daddy or of the fathers that we want, but
the dollar of the Yankee sons that the country requires ;
and that it ultimately must and will have, if it pro-
poses to prosper.

THE FALLACY OF A CHEAP CURRENCY.

But the advocates of the remonetization and ex-
tended use of silver as currency plant themselves on
what they regard as a fundamental axiomatic principle
—namely, that it is necessary and desirable to have a
cheap currency. But, as matter of fact, no commodity
currency (gold, silver, copper, iron, or cabbages) of one
kind can be relatively cheaper than one of another kind.
The value of each (if not a token currency, and minting
is free) will depend upon the amount of labor embodied
in or that will be required to purchase it: and no legislation can give to it any other value.   If a gold dollar cost
on an average one day's labor, and a silver dollar nine-
tenths of a day's labor, a dollar and ten cents of nominal
silver will sell for the same price as a dollar in gold.

Whatever nominal value, therefore, legislation may give to gold or silver, it will have no influence on the price of any commodity in the open (or world's) market. Neither gold nor silver can be made *fiat* money as to future transactions ; and the amount of labor expended in their production will establish their final and permanent value. If this value should fail to be recognized for a time, labor will go into other channels, and the production of these metals will cease until their labor value is again recognized.

NO NATIONAL ECONOMY IN RESTORING THE DOLLAR OF THE FATHERS.

As these truths are, however, persistently ignored by the majority of those who have undertaken to agitate for a renewed use of the dollar of the fathers, and as the force of the argument against the use of silver by reason of its cumbersomeness may be attempted to be met by assuming that it is proposed to use silver as a basis for the issue of a (paper) circulating medium, and not as a medium directly, it is desirable to still further elucidate this subject by illustration.

Thus, if it requires $500,000,000 to supply an exclusively gold currency for this country, and silver is depreciated ten per cent. in comparison with gold, it will require $550,000,000 in silver to perform the same work ; and it will require the same amount of commodities or embodied labor to buy the exclusively gold currency that it will to buy the exclusively silver currency. Whatever may be the dollar or the unit of coin adopted by any country, it will have no effect on future transactions, for prices will adapt themselves to the amount of labor embodied in the new coin, whether it be of great or small value, nominal or real. No one will be deceived by a mere nominal dollar. If it represents less embodied labor than the real dollar, it will depreciate just in proportion to the difference in the amount of labor embodied in the real and in nominal coin, and prices of every kind will advance just in proportion to the depreciation of the coin unit that is used. If the gold dollar should be made to contain double the amount of pure gold contained in the present dollar, prices, measured in dollars, would immediately depreciate one-half, and it would require only a mental operation to reduce the prices of commodities to the new standard. On the other hand, if a depreciated silver dollar currency should be adopted, it would only require a like mental effort on the part of the seller of property to advance his prices in proportion to the depreciation of the new coin, and no one would be deceived in either case. The aggregate nominal silver circulation would, however, be increased in proportion to the comparative depreciation of silver, and would cost in exchange for other products just the same amount as an aggregate gold circulation would cost. In other words, an exclusively aggregate gold currency can be bought as cheaply and with as little burden to the country as an exclusively aggregate silver currency, for they are both worth what they embody of labor—no more or any less on the average.

When the Connecticut Yankees counterfeited the wampum which Peter Stuyvesant made currency in New Amsterdam, it continued to depreciate in value until it sold at a price which barely remunerated the counterfeiters for its manufacture; and counterfeiting only ceased when the price, or exchangeable value, was reduced below the cost of its manufacture. If we permitted counterfeit notes to pass as legal tender, they would finally come down to represent the mere cost of the material of which they are composed, and of their manufacture, and would then become a commodity currency.

From these considerations, therefore, it would seem clear that there is nothing to be gained as to future transactions by having the coin currency of the country composed of one or the other of the two metals—gold or silver—except so far as one may have an advantage over the other in respect to convenience, adaptation to the business of the country—domestic and foreign—portability, and the like; and on all these points the balance of advantage for all transactions above $20 (a sum weighing more than a pound in silver) is largely on the side of gold; as will be evident when it is remembered that it requires sixteen times more time to count

2

silver in any considerable quantity than it does to count a like value in gold; sixteen times more strength to handle it; sixteen times more packages, casks or capacity to hold it, and sixteen times more expense to transport it. In other words, in this saving age, to use silver for large transactions, in the place of gold, is a misapplication and waste of fifteen-sixteenths of a given unit of effort, time, expense, and capacity, when one sixteenth would accomplish the same result.

SILVER INCONVENIENT BOTH FOR GENERAL CIRCULATION AND FOR BANK RESERVES.

Whatever coin is held as a reserve, or basis for banking, must at times be counted and at times transported from bank to bank, from city to city, from State to State, and from nation to nation. Bank notes must be redeemed somewhere and at some time, and if the redeeming coin is inconvenient for general circulation and inconvenient to handle, count, and transport, or to use as a bank reserve, its value as a redeeming coin will be diminished to the extent of all these inconveniences. The value of a redeeming currency consists largely in its adaptability to general circulation; but if the currency is bulky and ponderous, its value is diminished, because it is a constant menace to the creditor, who at the arbitrary will or caprice of the debtor, can be compelled to bring his wheelbarrow, cart, or freight-car, and receive the cumbersome coin. It may also be here pertinently asked, If silver is never to be counted, handled, weighed, or transported, why remove it from its native bed in the mines?

THE RELATIVE VALUE OF GOLD AND SILVER DETERMINED BY NATURAL AND NOT ARTIFICIAL LAWS.

One element of confusion that has been introduced in the recent discussions of the question of the use or disuse of silver as a material for currency has been the proposition soberly put forth, that the permanent and ultimate value of whatever is used as money depends on legislation; or, what is the same thing, that the value of a commodity can be established by law, and is not necessarily based upon the amount of labor employed in its production. But if all countries should demonetize both gold and silver, the market value of both metals must ultimately, by natural laws, be the same as now, when they are almost universally recognized as money. Universal demonetization would at first produce a surplus of the precious metals in form of coin. Production would cease—that is, the mines would be closed—and the coin in existence would finally be absorbed in the arts and for ornaments. Loss and abrasion would, however, continue, and at length new demands for the arts would arise, which could only be supplied by a remuneration for labor sufficient to induce a reopening of the mines, or what would be

equal to the remuneration obtained by following other
employments. When railroads replaced stage-coaches
there was in some sections of the country for a period a
surplus of coaches and horses. But natural laws in process of time restored the equilibrium, and now horses
and coaches cannot be bought at any less prices, or even
as cheap, as at the period when the displacement oc-
curred.

Silver is now depreciated probably by reason of
temporary causes. The drift of opinion with political
economists and those who have made the subject a
study, is that the present depreciation is not permanent, and has been produced mainly by the action
of certain of the governments of Europe demonetizing it, and forcing its sale as a commodity upon the
world's market. (From 1861 to 1873—year when the
German Government announced the demonetization
of silver—the variations in the market price of bar silver in the London market were between the limits of
60 5-16 and 61 11-16 per standard ounce.) At the present time the annual production of silver is less than
the annual product of gold; while the amount of silver
in existence in the world is conceded to be greater,
measured in dollars, than the stock of gold. (For 1876
the product of the mines of the United States was
$46,850,000 gold, and $38,500,000 silver. From 1860
to 1876 inclusive, the total product of our mines was
$766,777,000 gold and $289,854,000 silver.) All of the

more productive silver mines are now producing from
44 to 46 per cent. of gold in connection with silver;
and the improved machinery for working ores of silver
are equally applicable to the working of ores containing
gold, while one new process, largely profitable for the
working of gold—washing under hydraulic pressure—is
not at all applicable to the working of silver. Of course
it is not possible to foretell with certainty whether
silver may not be hereafter produced more abund-
antly and with less labor than at present, or formerly,
and less in proportion than is now required for the production of gold. But be this as it may, the amount of
labor expended in producing either metal in the future
must, as in the past, regulate the relative value of each.
If silver should cease to be a legal tender throughout
the world, it would still continue to be used as money,
until a substitute in the form of gold could be obtained.
Silver-coin is a non-perishable article, and the amount
of pure silver contained in such coin is well known. It
would, therefore, continue to be used at the convenience
of every community—at its market value in exchanges
—until an ample supply of the metal made legal tender
in the form of coin was obtained. Stage-coaches continue to be used after the introduction of railroads until
the supply and service of railroad cars are ample. The
theory, therefore, that the demonetization of silver will
produce a sudden vacuum of metallic currency, or a demand for gold, more than sufficient to cause its produc-

tion to the extent required, is chimerical and without foundation.

THE GOLD STANDARD OF THE COMMERCIAL WORLD A NECESSITY FOR THIS COUNTRY.

As already pointed out, the principal cause of the present depreciation of silver has been the discarding and sale of its silver currency by Germany; and as the great commercial nations of the world did not require this discarded silver, and would not purchase it for any purpose, depreciation has been the inevitable temporary result. The foreign commerce of the East Indies, to which countries the German silver must ultimately be exported, is limited; and these sections of the world, however much they may want silver, cannot suddenly receive and pay for large quantities of it. They must pay for what they receive with their exports, and these exports, with their limited foreign commerce, cannot be suddenly increased. But at the same time it is not improbable that the East, after a while, will absorb all the present apparent surplus silver of the West.

At present the East seems to require annually at least \$50,000,000 of silver* (for the years 1875–6, the exports from the West to the East exceeded \$75,000,000); and the present annual demand for the arts exceeds

---

* Mr. J. Hector, Deputy Secretary of the Bank of Bengal, has recently estimated that British India absorbed \$820,000,000 of silver in the twenty years prior to June, 1875, in excess of her exports of that metal.

$30,000,000. The present annual production of gold in the world exceeds $90,000,000. On the other hand, the present annual production of silver probably does not exceed $70,000,000. There is therefore nothing alarming in the present apparent abundant production of silver.

If now the United States should ally its destiny to a silver currency, and we should find at any time that we had an excess of silver, we should be in the present predicament of Germany — with no immediate purchaser or reservoir in the commercial world with which we have intimate relations to receive it, and should be under the necessity of trying to force it off through the narrow and gorged channels of East India commerce. We should be not less embarrassed if for any reason we needed suddenly an increased amount of silver; for then we should be obliged to draw it back through the same narrow and distant channels, requiring both time and expense.

WHY GIVE TO OTHER NATIONS AN OPTION TO TAKE OUR GOLD AT LESS THAN ITS VALUE IN THE WORLD'S MARKET?

Again, for the United States to now abandon the single and present exclusively gold standard and adopt the bi-metallic standard (both metals being made legal tender in the form of coin), would amount to practically giving to all the world the privilege of taking all our gold at a nominal price in silver, or all our silver at

a nominal price in gold. For arbitrarily fix what relations of value we will between gold and silver, there
will always be a liability to such changes in these relative values as to create an opportunity for a profit by
interchanging the one for the other in the form of coin,
the value of which has been arbitrarily established (tem-
porarily) by law. Now, what object can the people of
the United States have in giving to the rest of the
world such an option, when none of the commercial
countries with which we are on intimate commercial
relations propose to extend to us any such privilege?
The creating of conditions whereby such an option can
be given to foreign countries will unquestionably entail
upon us as a nation great inconveniences in the future,
as it has in the past. At times it may siphon out of the
country so much of our entire circulation as may be
silver and replace it by gold ; and at another time by
the change of temporary market values, or changes in
the legislation of other countries, the gold may be
siphoned out and the silver return. Any sudden influx
of foreign coin—gold or silver—would not, however, be
readily and at once practically available, as the people
would not at once willingly receive and admit the coins
of foreign nations into general circulation. But as the
capacity of our mints will be inadequate to meet these
extraordinary demands that may arise, the necessities
of the people may compel them to receive foreign coins
for a time, whose value they are incapable of suddenly

appreciating; thereby producing endless confusion and uncertainty, as was the case previous to 1853, when the country was flooded with old Spanish and Mexican depreciated coin, and when silver of American coinage of full legal weight flowed out of the country as fast as the mints could issue it. If France should admit free coinage and unrestrained circulation of silver, and silver continue depreciated, she would have to immediately mint anew not less than $700,000,000 of silver, which, by the competition of bullion brokers, would be sent to her in exchange and for the supplanting of the $700,000,000 of gold which she now possesses. This vast sum is more than sufficient for all the available silver in the world to cushion upon, if France should again adopt unlimited coinage of silver, and maintain her standard of 15½ to 1. Nor could we under such circumstances retain in this country a single dollar of silver, if it was remonetized here according to the standard of 16 to 1. In fact, with a bi-metallic standard we cannot control and say what kind of coin we will have in circulation ; for other countries can at their will draw from us either all our silver or all our gold, and substitute the one metal for the other. Long before we nominally demonetized silver it was practically demonetized and banished from our territory. The recent depreciation of silver is, however, due to the recent action of the German Government ; *and if any debtor, therefore, has now a grievance by reason of the demonetization of silver, it is a grievance against the German Empire and not against the Government of the United States.* Prudence, therefore, would seem to dictate that whether debtors have or have not a grievance, we should not again, by adopting the bi-metallic standard, permit the practical demonetization or monetization of either silver or gold in this country to be absolutely under the control of other governments. We cannot be masters of the situation with a bi-metallic standard. We can only control the kind of coin we will use by utterly refusing to give the option which the bi-metallic standard implies, and the real question of the whole controversy is, " Shall we have the coin of our choice or the coin which other nations may select to dole out to us as their caprice or interest may from time to time dictate? "

On the other hand, the great commercial countries with which we are in intimate relations, and which recognize the single gold standard, have great reservoirs of gold, and ability through their foreign commerce to either receive our surplus gold and pay for it or send us their surplus gold and receive our products in exchange. These great reservoirs of gold, furthermore, immediately respond to any deficiencies or demands for gold in the various commercial countries using gold as a standard, and so, by the law of supply and demand, keep the volume of gold in equilibrio with the volume of commodities to be measured, and greatly aid in maintaining, in respect to most articles, a uniformity of prices. It would seem to be apparent, therefore, from these considerations alone, that for this country to now reject the coin of the great commercial nations as a standard of value, and adopt another standard, or two standards, would inevitably entail upon it great and incalculable loss and inconvenience, and powerfully contribute to arrest our future industrial and commercial development.

THE DOLLAR OF THE FATHERS AND THE PAYMENT OF DEBTS.

The question of next and final importance to be considered is, Is it desirable to provide by legislation that debts incurred prior to 1873, when silver was demonetized, may be paid in either gold or silver, as the law authorized before that period? If silver is to be permanently and largely depreciated relatively to gold in consequence of a diminution in the amount of labor required to produce silver, this is a practical and important question of constitutional law and morals. But if the present price of silver is owing to the action of Germany, and if within a few years it is reasonably certain to resume its old price in the markets of the world; or if the adoption on the part of the United States of the bi-metallic standard will, as soon as our mints have coined all the silver presented for coinage, restore silver to par, or nearly par with gold, the question is comparatively unimportant. For the debtor cannot show that he has been injured unless he can prove that silver, as merchandise, would be depreciated, relatively to gold, after restoration of the bi-metallic standard as it existed at the time his debt was contracted. Let us, therefore, examine the question from the standpoint of constitutional law and morals.

Debts payable in coin are in effect payable in commodities. A coined dollar before 1873 in this country was not an imaginary unit, but a physical actuality composed of 412½ grains of silver, or 28.8 grains of gold. In all commercial transactions common honesty also requires that the dollar shall always be treated as a commodity—that is, that its name shall always indicate a given fineness and weight of metal. A bushel is not an imaginary measure of capacity ; a yard is not an imaginary measure of length ; a pound is not an imaginary measure of weight, and a dollar ought not to be regarded as in any sense an imaginary measure of value.

Again, debts payable in coin dollars are stipulated rights to specific property, and in both law and morals should be held equally sacred with property itself. Any interference with the rights of contracts is only a form of theft or robbery. It is true that there has never been any national law requiring that coin contracts shall be payable in gold and silver coins of the weight and fineness established by law at the time the contracts are made, but it is generally recognized, nevertheless, as a moral and constitutional obligation to pay in the same number of grains of pure metal as the law required when a given contract was made. And it is time that Congress should act and proclaim that this hereafter must be the known, conceded and recognized rule. There is no reason, furthermore, why this rule should not be applicable to all debts contracted when silver was a practical legal tender, even if silver is permanently depreciated, and if its full remonetization will not restore it to par with gold.

But conceding all this, it would be expedient for the debtor to inquire, whether he is to be in the least benefited by the proposed full and unlimited remonetization of silver. Let us, therefore, reason about this point a little.

DEBTS CONTRACTED SINCE 1873 SOLVABLE IN GOLD COIN.

Certainly it cannot be claimed that debts contracted *since* the demonetization of silver by Congress in 1873 are payable in any other coin than gold. And if it should appear that silver is permanently depreciated, it must be held that such debts can only be liquidated in gold or its equivalent. We say *must* because we assume that honesty is to be the supreme law of the land and that dishonesty is not to be tolerated.

It is now nearly five years since silver was nominally demonetized; and a large majority of the existing debts in the United States have been contracted in the mean-

time. But it is also true that silver has been practically demonetized in this country for more than forty
years, and at the time it was demonetized it was at a
premium in comparison with gold.

Now as to debts contracted when silver was practically demonetized. If we even admit that they are solv-
able in silver, but not at its market value at the time of
demonetization, in what manner will the debtor be
benefited by the privilege of using silver for his payments, if a full remonetization of silver will restore this
metal to its old status of about par with gold. The
debtor, then, cannot show that he has experienced a
grievance, unless he can also show that silver has been
permanently depreciated ; and that the present depreciation is not transient, arising from fluctuations in its
supply and demand, but from a permanent ability to
produce silver relatively to gold, cheaper than at any
former recent period. The future relation of silver to
gold if the United States should fully remonetize silver
is, to a great extent, a matter of conjecture ; but the in-
dications are, that silver after the full action of our
mints would be restored to about par in gold. The
country after the resumption of specie payments, will
require not less than 300,000,000 of coin. The re-adop-
tion of the bi-metallic standard, provided silver should
continue depreciated as an article of merchandise below
par in gold, would produce a demand for not less than
this full sum in silver. But where are 300,000,000 of

silver to be at once obtained? No government in
Europe, except Germany, owns a dollar of silver; and
the silver coin owned by individuals in European countries, unless silver is by the action of such countries demonetized, cannot possibly come here. Our standard of
16 for one, is about three per cent. higher than the standard of any country in Europe. The standard of European countries varies from 15–30 to 15–60, but at the
standard of 15–50, a citizen of France, where his silver
is a legal tender (but where the minting of silver is discontinued), would sustain a loss of three per cent. in
exchanging his silver for American silver; in addition
to commissions and expenses, which would be two per
cent. more, making a total loss on the whole transac-
tion of not less than five per cent. This is a practical
prohibition to the presentation of any European coined
silver held by individuals, to our mints for coinage.
Even the *five*-franc piece of France and of the Latin
union is now a token currency because it is a legal tender and its minting discontinued. France has no mo-
tive to demonetize her five-franc pieces, so long as they
are a mere token currency. Her statesmen know, if
they wish to get rid of them, that abrasion and loss
will, in time, absorb them. She has an abundance of
gold coin for all her international exchanges, and most
large business transactions. Prices are low in France
also, and by natural laws will absorb a large amount of
silver. Is it therefore probable that France will make

a sacrifice of five per cent. to get rid immediately, instead of by gradual absorption, of her five-franc token pieces? But if France should be willing to make such a sacrifice to get rid of her silver, what a warning it is to the United States against facilitating its reception in this country by inconsiderate legislation! Germany demonetized silver, because it was her exclusive legal-tender coin and which she found to be cumbersome in large transactions, especially in late years since the large advance in prices; and further because silver was not an international commercial coin, *i. e.*, a coin available for settling international balances. If Germany had possessed the bi-metallic standard and a fair supply of gold, it is not probable that she would have entirely demonetized silver; but would have permitted it to remain as a token currency, the same as France is now doing. It is apparent, therefore, that, the motives justifying Germany in demonetizing silver should influence the United States to refuse to remonetize it. The amount of silver that Germany has yet to throw upon the world's markets, is not probably in excess of $80,000,000. Holland has an exclusively silver currency, and may for the same reasons that have prompted Germany, follow her example and demonetize silver. But the available silver coin of Holland cannot exceed ten millions of dollars in amount; and this added to the stock which Germany can throw upon the market will make $90,000,000 or at the most $100,000,000 as the available silver of these two countries. It may be that there is another hundred millions of silver available from sources as yet not comprehended ; but as full remonetization of silver will certainly make an attraction here for $300,000,000, where will the last, or third hundred millions be obtainable, except in the East at rates about equal to par?

FULL REMONETIZATION OF SILVER AN INJURY, AND NOT A BENEFIT TO DEBTORS.

Remonetization of silver in the United States will, therefore, probably bring silver in proximity to par with gold in the open markets of the world, and it will in no way benefit the debtor if he counts as a benefit the opportunity to pay his debts in value less than he received. By the restoration of the bi-metallic stand-ard, also, the debtor will not be benefited, but is cer-tain to be materially injured. He will not obtain silver as money or merchandise at less than about par in gold, and he will thrust upon the community a currency cum-bersome to handle and use, an antiquated, inadequate tool of trade ; a coin that practically cannot be used in our international transactions ; and introduce a policy sure to hinder, if not arrest, the revival of business and national industrial and commercial development. And the burden of all these evils will fall alike upon the debtor and creditor. In short, for the debtor to advo-cate remonetization of silver, or the restoration of the bi-metallic standard, is to play the part of the Greek fool who, sitting upon a limb, sawed it off between himself and the trunk of the tree.   Up to the present time the main effect of the demonetization of silver has been to deprive Germany of the opportunity of selling her cumbersome silver, and dumping it at par on to this country: and to ask this nation to now remonetize silver is, in effect, asking us to go into the " old clo' " business, and array ourselves in old garments which other nations are anxious to discard, and pay for such garments the full price of new clothes.

THE ADOPTION OF THE BI-METALLIC, OR ALTERNATE STANDARD IS A VIOLATION OF THE NATURAL LAW OF SUPPLY AND DEMAND, WHEN ONE COIN IS MORE CONVENIENT THAN THE OTHER.

It is claimed by some, that the demonetization of silver, and the adoption of a single gold standard, will so far appreciate the price and value of gold, as to greatly increase the burden of existing debts, and diminish the supply of useful instrumentalities for effecting national exchanges.   But this, although a specious, is an utterly false theory, unsustained by either facts, or logic.   Any demand, where human industry is left free, will be met by a corresponding supply.   The fact that there may be at a given time an increased demand for gold, and a diminished demand for silver, does not necessarily indicate or prove, that the cost in labor of producing gold has increased, or the cost of producing silver has decreased. It simply indicates the direction that natural laws are giving to production, and also that the same laws are interposing obstacles in the way of producing things inconvenient or useless. It is undoubtedly true that the cost of producing both gold and silver is much less than formerly. Every railroad and other modern improvement, which gives cheaper clothing and food to miners, as well as all labor-saving machinery employed in mining, enables labor to produce a larger amount of gold and silver in a given time. Hence the great depreciation of both gold and silver during the last third of a century. And the probabilities are that this depreciation in the value of this precious metal will further continue ; and creditors must submit to such results. Within the next quarter of a century, instead of one railroad crossing our continent, there will probably be half a dozen, with several branches, further developing our natural reservoirs of gold and silver. In fact the recent abundant, or, what is the same thing cheap production of both gold and silver, is the sole cause which has necessitated the partial demonetization of silver—the most cumbersome metal—by countries maintaining a high scale of prices of wages and commodities. In other words, it is the abundance, not scarcity, of the precious metals that has given rise to the controversy as to what metals it is expedient to use at this time for circulating media. No one can suppose that this controversy about demonetization of silver has been occasioned by any abstract desire for discussion; it has been forced on the world by the necessities of the situation. There is a natural law by which both labor and capital tend to the most profitable employments, and if there is a temporary increased demand for gold and a temporary diminished demand for silver, labor and capital in the production of gold will be supplemented, until an equilibrium is established, and without any reference to the permanent cost of the production of either metal. Supply and demand are to production what waves are to the ocean; and notwithstanding the depressions created always and everywhere by these waves, all scientists agree that the general and average level of the ocean is constant and unvarying. It is by the natural laws of supply and demand that the introduction of the most desirable commodities is always stimulated, and the production of surplus and unsuitable articles is checked and discouraged, without reference to their cost of production. It has also been before pointed out, that the cost of producing silver relatively to gold has not been apparently diminished. Now, applying these principles to the problem under consideration, it follows that the adoption of the bi-metallic or alternate standard may, for a period, create an artificial demand for a coin not suited to the wants of some communities, the result of which may be the indefinite production of an article not well suited to certain human wants. Nature has created an abundance of both gold and silver. If man refuses to produce the metal best adapted to his wants, and persists in producing another, ill-adapted to his wants, by an artificial, bi-metallic standard, he makes warfare upon the beneficence of the Almighty. Therefore the conclusion:—that the adoption of a bi-metallic standard is a violation of the natural laws of supply and demand, and an attempt to provide for the survival of unfittest.

Again, the gold-producing power of the earth is abundant and unlimited, and the supply of this metal will be no more limited in the future, than the supply of milk or whiskey; and if left to natural laws will always be equal to the demand. The employment of coin is not an absolute necessity, for commerce can be carried on by barter. But food and clothing are absolutely necessary for the sustenance of human beings. And yet we find that these absolutely necessary articles are best supplied when their production is left to the natural laws of supply and demand. Value is the relation or ratio between two articles or services ; and there is no more propriety in establishing a relation between silver and gold, than between iron and lead, or rye and wheat ; or between silver or gold and brass, copper and all other commodities. When economic laws, and the efficacy and value of individual judgment were less understood than now, governments were logical, and established prices, or the relations of all labor or commodities to gold and silver. But now, in the main, prices and production are left to individual judgment and competition, and an arbitrary regulation of the relations of silver to gold is now the sole relic of governmental interference in regulating the prices of articles; or, in other words, in establishing the relation of things as expressed in money. The reason why gold and silver are the best standards of value is, that they are the products of human labor, and that their production will always be regulated by demand. They are, therefore, not a *fiat* currency. The quantity produced is not regulated by the arbitrary actions of any government, but is determined by individual judgment and the natural influence of competition. The production of gold in the United States is at present between forty and fifty millions per annum, or some ten millions in excess of the annual production of silver. There is no reason why this domestic product of gold should not be augmented to more than one hundred millions per annum, if there is a demand for it—and all there is wanting to produce it, is demand. We have capital and abundance of labor craving employment, and gold-bearing rocks and fields without limit. Here is an unlimited opportunity for debtor or creditor who wants to root or labor at the remuneration of other similar labor; and it is not proposed to compel him to root or labor at something that is less profitable. Again, if it is gold rather than silver that is wanted in this country, every pound of our silver product, as well as our other commodities, can be used to buy gold in the markets of the world: and thus the gold resources of the world are at our command.

CONCLUSION.

There can be no objection to the use of silver as a subsidiary or token currency, issued only in exchange for gold at nominal values, or at all times redeemable in gold at nominal value, not legal tender in excess of $20 for any one specific payment, to any extent the people will desire. But when it is proposed to go further, and compel the sons to accept the dollar of the fathers to an unlimited amount, then an answer to this proposition, simple and conclusive, is that the dollar of the fathers is not, on grounds of convenience, adapted to our use. The "sons" want something better—the most improved tools of trade—as they want better methods of conveyance, of warming, of lighting, ventilation, printing and communication of news, than did the fathers. They want, as a condition for success in business, the coin receivable without discount by the great commercial nations with which the bulk of our foreign commerce is conducted. And herein is another point that ought not to fail of receiving full consideration, namely, that whereas, in most cases, the first cost of an improved tool is greater at the outset than that of a poor and unimproved one, in this case the

conditions are reversed ; for the first cost of the good
tool—a gold currency—will be no greater at the out-
set to the country than the first cost of the poor one—
a silver currency; while in all subsequent respects the
advantages are immeasurably in favor of the gold. We
have, furthermore, no embarrassing antecedents in the
way of our adoption of the best machinery of trade.
We have an inconsiderable amount of silver in the
country, and it would seem the height of folly to
adopt a currency not receivable by the commercial
countries with which we sustain the most intimate relations, and objectionable on the score of convenience
and the changed condition of the times. If we were
overloaded and crowded with a depreciated silver currency we might decline to abandon it: refusing, however, to mint any more, and making what exists, until
lost or destroyed, a mere token currency :—thus imi-
tating the example of France. But having the opportunity to start fresh, and, as it were, from the beginning,
is it not clearly the correct public policy to adopt a
coin currency suited to our wants and the age? Any
attempt to restore the old silver dollar to its place
as lawful money, without qualification or limitation, is
as foolish and absurd as an attempt to displace through
legislation railroads by stage-coaches, and steamships
by sailing-vessels. Sovereign power can violate natural
laws, the same as individuals can : but the penalty of
violation is inevitable in both cases.

REPUDIATION.

THE REPEAL OF THE RESUMPTION ACT ENTAILS AN
OBLIGATION TO PAY INTEREST ON THE LEGAL-TENDER
NOTES AFTER JANUARY 1st, 1879.

Can the obligations of the Resumption Act be constitutionally repealed or questioned?

The Resumption Act provides that, "on and after
the 1st day of January, 1879, the Secretary of the
Treasury shall redeem in coin the United States legal-
tender notes then outstanding, on their presentation
for redemption, at the office of the Assistant Treasurer
of the United States, in the city of New York, in sums
of not less than fifty dollars." This is a plain and
distinct obligation, which runs with every legal-tender
note as a negotiable instrument,—the evidence of a
liquidated sum,—and which cannot be violated without
a plain and distinct violation of the 4th section of the
14th article of the Federal Constitution, which declares
that "*the validity of the public debt of the United States
authorized by law, shall never be questioned;*" nor can
any member of Congress, it would seem, vote for the

repeal of the Resumption Act without violating his oath to support the Constitution, and committing an open act of repudiation, unless some other method of redemption, or payment, is previously adopted and willingly accepted by the holders of the legal-tender.

Futhermore, can the holders of legal tender—a recognized and liquidated debt—be constitutionally coerced to extend the time of their redemption beyond January, 1879, without payment of interest on such deferred payment? Lord Mansfield, in one of the standard English cases (2 Burr, 1077, 1086), lays down what may be considered as a recognized legal axiom. "Where money," he says, "is made payable by an agreement between parties, and a time given for the payment of it, this is a contract to pay the money at the given time, and to pay interest from the given day, in case of a failure of payment at that day." In the case of Thorndike v. United States (Mason, p. 1) the United States Circuit Court (Justice Story) held, that a Treasury (United States) note, payable in one year with interest, draws interest until paid by the government "in the same manner as a private contract." And in the case of Erskine v. Van Arsdale (15 Wallace, p. 77) the United States Supreme Court (Chief-Justice Chase) said, "the ground for the refusal to allow interest [on the part of the United States] is the presumption that the government is always willing and ready to pay its ordinary debts." By all rules of law, business

precedents, and precepts of morality, therefore, the
Federal Government, in case of unwillingness, inability,
or failure to pay or discharge its obligations at an
agreed time, is obligated and must be considered to
have contracted to pay interest from the date of such
failure or inability. The date of payment is obviously
of the essence of the contract. The refusal to pay at
maturity a six per cent. promise, for a period of sixteen
years, is equivalent to a repudiation of a sum equal to
what was originally promised.

Failure to pay is either temporary suspension or
bankruptcy; but in a case of temporary suspension,
debts by universal law and practice, draw interest from
the date of non-payment. Now if from any cause the
government shall be unable to meet its negotiable and
adjusted obligations on the 1st of January, 1879, the obligation to pay interest from the date of failure would
be in full force and effect (the same as in a private
contract), and the validity of this obligation, according
to the Federal Constitution, cannot be questioned.
Clearly, therefore, there is no alternative for the government on the 1st of January, 1879, but to either redeem its
notes, or pay an acceptable rate of interest upon them,
or go into bankruptcy and unconstitutional repudiation.
Fortunately for the country, the constitutional amendments forever prohibit repudiation ; and it is fortunate,
likewise, that President Hayes, in his letter of acceptance
as a candidate for the Presidency, has clearly expressed

his firm conviction that constitutional obligations and national honor requires that all national obligations, including legal-tender notes, must be paid according to existing law. He says: "*I regard all the laws of the United States relating to the payment of the public indebtedness, the legal-tender notes included, as constituting a pledge and moral obligation, of the government, which must in good faith be kept.*" And no true American, jealous of the honor of his country, a supporter of the Federal Constitution, and a believer in the sacredness of contracts, can, it would seem, do otherwise than demand that the Resumption Act be carried out, and support the President in case of the contingency of a veto of any Congressional enactment looking to postponement or repeal of the promise of resumption. ·

If from any cause the Treasury is unable to redeem legal tenders at the designated time, it is certainly competent for Congress, and also its duty, to order the notes presented for redemption to be stamped, and bear the current rate of interest from the day of demand. This is the legal, constitutional and honest course, unless we propose to walk in the path of repudiation. Will it be pretended that the obligation to pay interest on an overdue negotiable legal-tender note of the government is any less binding than on an overdue negotiable bond? Will any one assume that government has the right to postpone the payment of an overdue bond without payment of interest on the same? There is an old maxim equally applicable to government as to individuals, "that there is no person so poor that he cannot give his note with interest for his debts."

The propriety of funding, prior to 1879, legal-tender notes in given or unlimited amounts, has been suggested as an aid to resumption, and such a measure may be considered desirable. But it must be evident, if the analysis of the law and the co-relative provisions of the Constitution as above given be correct, that the government has already agreed in the Resumption Act to fund, or, what is equivalent, to pay interest on any part of the legal-tender notes, which it may fail to redeem on presentation at the time and place specified. The Redemption Act is, therefore, equivalent to a funding act under certain circumstances.

It is not probable, however, that a contingency of a default on the part of the government under the Redemption Act can occur. The Secretary of the Treasury has been given ample powers to "prepare" for resumption before the 1st of January, 1879, and to "provide" for resumption after that date. He is authorized to sell bonds to any extent necessary to carry the act into effect, bearing 4, 4½, or 5 per cent. interest, at his discretion. Five per cent. bonds are far above par now; and will undoubtedly command par in gold on and after January, 1879, if the policy of the government is free from all taint of repudiation. Under such a condition of things there is no way to prevent redemption under existing laws except for Congress to propose or enact measures injurious to the credit of the government. For if an unexpected amount of legal-tender notes should be presented at a given day for redemption, beyond the amount of coin at the imme-diate command of the Treasury, the credit of the gov-ernment being unimpaired, the sale of bonds would pro-ceed; giving ample means, within a brief period, for a renewed redemption; and thus after redemption once commences it must go on, as it were, automatically; the legal-tender notes, by the circuitous action of the sale of the bonds for gold, and the exchange of legal-tender notes for gold, being practically convertible into a five per cent. ten year gold bond, if the government cannot obtain gold at a less rate.

The issue before Congress and the nation is, then, as follows : redemption under the present act, payment of interest from date of default, or repudiation to the ex-tent of the interest refused ; and repudiation cannot be brought about without positive measures on the part of Congress, which are sure to be alike condemned by the veto of the Executive and the judgment of the country.

The apprehension of the country in respect to the effects of specie resumption suggests the story of the man who, walking one evening in a deserted mining region, fell into a pit. Grasping, however, as he fell, a projecting root, he hung suspended in the dark over what he regarded as a terrible abyss, until his strength failed him, when, saying his prayers, repenting of his sins, and commending his soul, he let go and fell—*about six inches.* His hair, nevertheless, is said to have turned white. If specie payments, by resolute, determined effort, were to be brought about to-morrow, everybody, the next day, would draw a long breath, and involuntarily exclaim, "Is that all?" And the day after they would begin to ask, "Wherein is the benefit?" The benefit would not be seen at once; natural prosperity will not come back through resumption alone. But it would be as in the case of a workman who exchanges a bad tool for a good one. He would recognize the benefit of the exchange when he began to work, and found he could do more and better work, and with less effort, with the new tool than he could with the old.—*Extract from article "Resumption of Specie Payments," in North American Review, November, 1877, pp.* 408–412. *Opinion of David A. Wells.*

www.ingramcontent.com/pod-product-compliance
Lightning Source LLC
Chambersburg PA
CBHW021547270326
41930CB00008B/1395